PROV

Poems

Rick Campbell

[handwritten inscription]

Stan — you have
Been there with
me from the
Beginning —
10/25/20

BLUE HORSE PRESS   REDONDO BEACH, CALIFORNIA   2020

PROVENANCE

Poems

Rick Campbell

Blue Horse Press
Redondo Beach,
California

Cover photo: "Alligator Point, FL." Rick Campbell ©
Used by permission
Internal photos are credited to the author

Editors: Jeffrey and Tobi Alfier
Blue Horse Press logo: Amy Lynn Alfier (1996)

ISBN 978-0-578-76398-9

FIRST EDITION © 2020

This and other Blue Horse Press Titles may be found at
www.bluehorsepress.com

This is my seventh book of poetry. I hope there will be more, but it seems that this is a good time and place to thank people—teachers, friends, editors—who have had a hand in making all of this possible. Starting at the beginning—Daniel Scott, Lawrence Hetrick, Rhonda Riley, Brandy Kershner, Stephen Corey, Van K. Brock, Ralph Berry, Lynne Knight, Judith Kitchen, Frank X. Gaspar, Philip Levine, Michael Simms, Bob Kunzinger, Lisa Zimmerman, and Donna J. Long.

Bob Dylan, John Prine and a number of other great songwriters must be thanked too.

And, as always, this collection is dedicated to my daughter, Della Rose Campbell.

Acknowledgements

I'd like to thank the following publications where these poems have appeared or will appear.

Aethlon: "Walk Off"
Alabama Literary Review: "Waiting for Everyman," "What I Might Want Today," "Reckoning."
Black Phoenix: "Seashore"
Chasing Light (Yellow Jacket Press): "Ybor City on a Friday."
Congeries: "Hay Bales on the Northern Plains," "Selling My Dead Brother"
Dash: Literary Journal: "Song for Jasper at Fernandina Beach."
Free State Review: "Smack in the Middle of Nowhere." "The Power of the Visible Bought in a Used Bookstore."
Gargoyle (forthcoming): "Ash," "Burning the Railroad Tracks," "Forgetting the Nicene Creed."
The Georgia Review: "My Detroit."
Kestrel: A Journal of Literature and Art: "Dates, A Meditation, 2015."
Lightning Key" "Cats on the Road."
Prairie Schooner "In Cheyenne I Consider My Father in Surgery."
Snakebird 2019, (Anhinga Press). "An Abundance of Caution," "The World Can Break Your Heart with Its Forever."
Sweet: A Literary Confection (forthcoming): "Parable of the Forest Pygmy"

Contents

Prose Poems

This is the story of how we begin to remember.

— Paul Simon

In the Long Dark West of Fargo

Here, we are on the earth: large, distant.
Plains, buttes, bluffs stretch beyond
what eyes can see. Should the wind we know
waits roar and blow, all of this, train too
would be lost in the blizzard's maw.
Even in such desolation, I know where we are going.
Havre, Cutbank, Browning, Whitefish, Libby.
Years ago I lived in these towns and rivers when I rose
from an eddy to snatch a fly and discovered what might be.
Mission Creek running hard for joy, trout
asleep under Kapowsin ice, what he said
the Indians knew about death. He's not here.
Let's not get carried away. This isn't a séance.
Crusted snow edges station tracks gray.
I'm crossing Montana, heading west on the Empire
Builder to where the Stilli, Skagit and Hoh
fall every day to the sea.

My Detroit

after Phil Levine

One night we drove my baby
blue Falcon from the Valley
across Ohio and Indiana, which
none of us remembered, into
Detroit. Two white kids
and K; we went where
he said. Turned here. Parked there.
We didn't know, knew we
shouldn't speak until spoken
to, and even then, softly. K
and some guy left the apartment
with our combined fortunes
and someone gave us
a gun—dark, oily.
M held it then passed it to me
like a baby. I slid it under
a green suede pillow
and we watched the door someone
might come through, someone
the gun was meant to stop. Night
crawled on until K came
back with a grocery bag of weed.
I slid the pillow off the pistol
and walked out into the street
of yellow light. What street we
never knew; whose Detroit
we could not guess. Not ours.
Three in the morning Detroit's empty
as everywhere else. We drove

wired on black beauties
and not dying. The sun rose
south of Cleveland. Levine said Detroit
in '82 taught him that "nothing lasts." For us,
it was enough that it was there.

What a small great blessing
it is, when you're twenty,
to live as if every door is safe, every
street unarmed, and every
highway takes you home.

The Dark Angel: Iowa City, (October 2009)

                                    for R.P.

Not the Grievous Angel Gram Parsons
sang of, though this stone too has grief
as its provenance. So many have come here
and sat beneath its stubbed wings—many drunk,
some sober, some with questions, some with answers
we can likely figure wrong.
                         Here you found yourself
parsing poetry with Lowell and Berryman, practicing
what you had to say. Orphan boy, lost
man, adrift on the prairie, too far
from Cape Cod to go back to what was
always lost and home. This is why
some of us need angels, some whiskey,
                              some smack.

You grew tired as we shuffled
to the angel. Death trailed behind us.
In the afternoon's gray and coming cold
did your angel whisper something I couldn't hear?
As we drove out of town, fields
were brown and brown some more.

4

In Cheyenne I Consider My Father in Surgery

Wide streets, few trees. Cowboy
boots in the windows. Dust
in the wind smacks like gravel, wearing
down enamel and desire. Trash flies
low like scavenger birds. We park.
Look for beer. I'm wondering
about that knife in your heart, chest
cracked open, spread bone to bone,
like an angel spread-eagled, staked
down, waiting its due. What do they
do with all the blood? It's been too
long. I don't care. She thinks I should.
I think I should. The jukebox
disappoints me. No Bob Wills,
no Orbison or Buddy Holly. Dance
floor's a hundred feet deep and empty
as a grade school on a Saturday.
Rodeo days long gone. How
can lovers drink here
after the stars fall down?
They cut you. It's routine.
You ought to be alive, but this
far away, I don't know. Wind
rocks the truck. My knuckles
white on the wheel. Snow
on the Front Range will blow
down through Laramie tonight.
I love to watch her undress. Small waist,
sweet breasts, long black hair. We
have a bed on the floor.
You don't know where I live.

Ash

After G.L.

I am not Ash,
though I am of ash from J&L Steel,
ARMCO, American Bridge—breathed, seeped
through pores, swallowed with my bread.

Ash, ashes,
soot, the valley tattooed our bodies.
Ash in our air, ash in our taps,
ash in our bath; ash in our gutters,
in the cracks of our sidewalks. Ash
smeared cars, windows, the siding
added to our houses. Ash
rain darkened the stained glass
of St. Joseph's Catholic Church
where ash coated pews, the collection
basket, our mumbled prayers.

In the sixties
old folks told us of days when the sun
did not shine. Streetlights blotted out.
Our grandparents, blurs going to work,
coming home, promises that we would one day
be born, grow up and find our way out of here.

Until then
I marked my name on surfaces supposed to shine—
our car, strangers' cars parked silently near
the curb—as I walked to church. I broke
the brown crusted snow to search
for the clean and white below.

Burning the Railroad Tracks

40 below, ropes doused in kerosene
blaze down the tracks, parallel
into the dark future. You
can ride this train blind, ride
your sins long past penance,
to Fargo, Grand Forks, even Bemidji,
that place in your soul where
you wake with a crow staring into
your blinking eyes. On any small rise
you can see straight to Canada.
The fiery tracks, real or imagined,
show you the way to Winnipeg
if you're fool enough to go.

Meditation on the Bower's House Trees

North of Athens, I'm troubled that I don't know
the names of these green and waxy trees.

Bamboo in the side yard seems out of place too.
I'm a stranger here, crossed too many

fauna lines. Thirty miles north,
mountains rise above Toccoa.

I know little about tolerance and range,
but I believe that like us trees might find themselves

far from where seed books label home. Banana tree
in afternoon sun, sheltered from north wind.

Its fruit grows wild, small,
               never ripens.

Ybor City on a Friday

> So high the street girls wouldn't take my pay
> They said come see me on a better day
> She just danced away
>
> Jason Isbell

I've never had a street girl, high
or straight. Never a drug habit,
not a drunkard either. I have no
indecent crutch for my failures.
I've studied most sins at a distance.
In this new old age if I'm a tattered
man on a stick, I've come here
through my own neglect. On this bench
I watch the street girls. They know
I can't pay. Still, they smile. Our hearts
go out to each other like pigeons
picking the park clean. Blessed
are warm nights. Cursed the rain
and mosquitoes. The understory
below the banyan feels safe—though
rats and roaches rattle thick leaves
like those punk bullies who cruise
the park at night. I would die
in Pittsburgh, bent into a corner door.
We know to come south: new era
pioneers, not looking for the Dream
just to sleep and wake when the street
cars clack past. The gas company
lights are stars in a heaven
we'll find wanting someday.

Hay Bales on the Northern Plains

I want them to be buffalo, huddled
within their shaggy selves under winter
sky almost white as snow below, buffalo
that survived the long rifles and chant
Buffalo Bill's dead as each observation car passes.

Beyond this pasture everything blurs
to obscure—North Dakota stretching
north to Canada. Where are we?
Not the Badlands, not good lands either.
Soon, spring; this might be green
wheat. Another season, harvesters

dusting the air gold. Already
diligent farmers have ploughed
curved furrows. My train rolls through
last February days, Fargo to Minot,
Minot to Williston's fracking camps.
Last night I slept, twisted, covered
by my jacket and dreamed of Key West.

Now I'm humming Marley. Bleak
seems overused. White's inadequate.
Think of the Whale, the Eskimo's hundred names
for snow. I am out of my land, sky not mine,
air fierce and frigid. These late years, it takes
more and more to redeem my solitary man.

Imagined buffalo, glimmer of blue sky,
brief swatch of a field not cut to stubble,
Minot's promise of a fast walk to a bad cup of coffee's
not enough. Tomorrow, from the rapids
                              to the sea.

Song for Jasper at Fernandina

I have a bird that whistles,
a bird that sings. Stole that line
from the blues. I don't have a bird.
I have a dog who neither sings nor whistles,
but he would herd cattle if we
had some. He's from Australia
back in his dog days, some ancestral
down under where dingoes howl
at the moon of his dreams. Jasper,
my mate. Today, he said no to the Atlantic
waves breaking on the beach. *Cattle dog,*
he said, and lunged for the steps to the big house
behind the dunes. Not that one, I said,
they say John Grisham lives there.
I whistle show tunes, blues, Shenandoah.
We cross the highway and work
our way to the green grass shoulder,
a place to squat. Grisham
writes about lawyers, I say.

Blue

Blue springs, Blue, bluer, bluest. Blue firmament.
Blue as sapphire. "The ladies were very blue
and well informed." Blue-billed, blue-
bloused, blue-breasted. Am I Blue?
Blue Angel, blue ash. Blue-eyed Mary. Blue
Joe, Blue John, Blue Johnny, Blue Lucy, Blue-
winged shoveller?

The Saint Johns, more a string of ponds
and marshes than river, dribbles north
from Vero, from Lake Wales Ridge through Lake
Hell'n Blazes, through poinsettias, Tarzan's
abandoned Rhesus monkeys wailing the moon
will hide its light when you get the blues
                                        in the night.

Don't it make your brown eyes blue? Blue Velvet,
Blue Suede Shoes, Blue Moon of Kentucky, Blue
Eyes Crying in the Rain. Blue Monday. My Blue
Heaven. "The last time I saw you looked so much older
your famous blue raincoat was torn at the shoulder."
Once in blue moon a river flows north—Sanford,

Palatka, Green Cove Springs, Orange Park,
Jacksonville, the sea. Flat land, tide pulses inland.
Blue river running slow and lazy.
Where does this begin?

Think of Bartram on the water, pirogue
besieged by alligators. His campfire
blazing to drive them away. A man will sweet
talk. A man will ....

Bartram saw mullet fly through the sky, tumble
like acrobats as they fell back to the river.
There's no river here unless we make it.
Blue, songs are like tattoos. Blue
I love you. I was young when L. wrote
"Sandhills and rivers what we know.
My life is broken. And so."

Blue river's origin in the blue moon's
eye. On the river's banks many settlements,
simple, unchanging, visceral, ephemeral.
Building, wasting, resurrecting. Dying,
being born. Loving.

Blue is the color of my true love's eyes. How
is this theft, dear one? I write to you from what
some in the village would call wilderness.
La Florida. Snakes and alligators sleep and I dream
of you. Dear One, I could tell you that I've found
the spring of Provenance and say it's blue as my heart's

many desires sparkling in the water over the low rail
of my shallow boat. Dear One, I could sink to the bottom
with the silver fish that dart in and out of green grass,
if not for you. Winter would hold no spring.

The Blue Heron stalks in cypress shadows, silent and still
as blue night falling. Dear One, I would be the mullet,
except for the locket you tied to my journal, now so tangled
up in blue. Canopy so thick here, everything is dark. Bluer
than the blue devils, bluer than your pale blue angel.

Father, mother, brother, dead.
Blue ruin takes me home.

Things I Learned from my Map on the Kitchen Wall

That Pittsburgh is east of Palm Beach,
and Tallahassee below Detroit. That New
Jersey's near the same latitude as middle Nebraska,
and San Antonio, which I always thought
"out west," isn't. The 100th parallel is easy to see.
There's nothing much there—no cities, few rivers.
The line cuts south through what early settlers called
barren, then Dodge City, its westernness iconic,
Matt Dillon etched in my baby boomer mind.
Now I know it sits on the western edge
of the Midwest, though who quibbles
about the town where cattle were sent to die
and Kitty was a madam with a heart of gold.
Longitude lines bend more east and west
of the 100th parallel, making Cape Mendocino appear
farther west than Cape Blanco, where Michael
rolled down the great dune and the humpback
eyed him not more *than a damned plug's cast offshore.*
Straight meridians are false as the flat earth
we could have fallen off, until Columbus, Magellan
and all the sailors without names didn't.

Early Morning on the Porch with L&C

Had Breakfast. Listen to bird
drone and echo. In the distance
cars rumble up and down Tharpe St.
Third cup of coffee, the raccoon
walks noisily out of the green hedge
to eat the almost-stray cats' food
on the carport floor. The raccoon's
wary of me here, sitting, reading, writing,
but he settles in. I think of running him off,
but hell, it's just cat food. There's thirty more
pounds in the closet and thousands at the store.

L&C trade trinkets to the Nez Pierce as a down
payment on Idaho. Beyond the backyard wall
of magnolia and live oak hung with moss
and twisted vines, I hear geese honking. It's time
for them to head north. The raccoon will eat
until all the food's gone; he does not gulp
He's not wild in his habits, doesn't hoard
like fat squirrels down from barren fig and pine.
When he's done, he's gone. Clark's been sick
a lot on the cold Lolo Crossing. Eating dogs
bought from the Shoshone and roots
he has no name for. He eats & pukes
      & is much relieved.

Cats on the Road

for Sylvan, for Lisa

The cats only cried to Laramie
and then settled down; the long ride
became one of their nine lives seeping through
the thin membrane that separates lives
and possibly love and disaster—the wreck

on the highway, not Roy Acuff's high twang,
but four semis jackknifed, twisted, the last,
cab crushed and singing *death played her hand*
in destruction, but I didn't hear nobody pray.
The cats were sleeping, but she shuddered

the next hundred miles, a waking dream, steel
cascading over the road like coffee spilling
from an overturned cup. Somewhere
in Western Idaho the cats knew
this was a new life and woke to plot

how they'd explore the corners of strange rooms,
how to play in light flecked with humidity, how
soft the bed would be without the dry charge
they'd always known. They dreamed
of the long days' naps to come, and there was nothing

for cats to cry about anymore. Eugene came up green—
fir and spruce. Cats looked out the window
as the truck slowed from interstate's hum
to the bounce and jangle of the street. We
are home they said. Soon, the phone rang
and she said *yes. Yes.*

Walk Off

That afternoon you came back from work
I was stretched on your couch watching
the Pirate's game as if this was our life.

I wanted to be your coach, explain balk,
hit & run, fielder's choice, and chin music.
When you found yourself driving dark

curves home and the radio sang
there's a long drive to right over the Clemente wall,
a walk off home run for Jones, I wanted you

to think of me and what all of this means,
a rare steal of home, here
in the dark, far from stadium lights.

Cooking My Dinner with Glenn Miller

My mother's old electric skillet, dial stuck
on high, sizzles mushrooms, onions and peppers.
A squeaky tape plays *Glen Island Special's*
high hat snare. He was my mother's favorite.
She graduated the summer war came calling,
danced to *Moonlight Serenade*. Her beau
joined the Air Force, and she, a secretarial school
in Charlestown. *Wistful and Blue* was Top Ten.

Sun Valley Jump hit the charts as Churchill
tried to hold the good world together. FDR
knew we were sliding, but not how fast
the slope; he had eyes on the Germans
as the Japanese came out of the sun. My
mother did her part—cutting off lights,
rationing fuel, sending boxes to her boys.

Thirty years after *Here We Go Again*
we watched football as she fried chicken
in a trailer in the South Florida sun,
one palm tree shading nothing,
fan big as an airboat roaring hot air down
the narrow hallway. The boy who danced
with her Charlestown nights flew a B-17
that never came home.

Winter Night

We stare past each other. Me, at something
distant, trying to be outside this house,
maybe rolling down the hill, a body

in motion pulled ineluctably away
like flotsam in the Atlantic current.

I don't want to have a choice about leaving.
I want to blame this on circumstances, obligation,
duty, necessity. On what any good father would do.

I want to have been a good father. When? When we look
back and take stock? Now? I want to wash my hands

like Pilate but there's no scapegoat. You sit
and stare past your lap at the table leg. It's fat
near the top, lathed thinner, like a woman's waist

in the middle, then wide again like her hips.
You're not going anywhere. Not looking for absolution,

for someone or something to blame. Our river
eddies and flows around you. A cartographer
could say this river joins a river, then another river,

then the sea, but that's not the end, just a change in elements,
part and parcel. The river becomes part of something larger—
air, cloud, planet, galaxy, cosmos, the body of a god, a goddess,

their bodies united. If all this tonight were just metaphysics,
easy or hard speculation, and I were trying to say this

is just a bad moment in a river of days, that we,
bodies in motion being pulled apart, will be pushed
together again. If I were trying to say I'm sorry—

this silence, this dark December night works against
my lackadaisical theory. Proof?

I believe there will be one, but that's faith,
and faith, if you need it to prove your love,
is not what we made faith for.

Tropical Storm in the Gulf

Birds in the trees rattle the coming
of the morning freight. Rain
running off my sheet metal roof

floods the parking lot. My daughter
sleeps under loblollies forty miles
away. When Adam and Eve

stood outside Eden's gate
did they hope, despite being God's
first creation, that someone out there

would be willing to open a door,
lay down a mat, offer a bowl of stew.
By now there have been so many beginnings.

Soon she'll wake into this last summer
before the world lays full claim
on her. Wind stings my face.

Tense

My mother is dying—this is a problem
of tense. My mother is dead
and I am on the couch remembering.
Three dogs wait with me for dawn.

My mother is still dying.
When the sun rises
over the loblollies, my dogs
explore night's changes,

wander, noses in pine straw
smelling the new morning
earth armadillos dug. Run
through dying winter rye

tracking rabbits and deer through
the beans and tomatoes. And
still my mother is dying.
I'm surrounded by books.

On the flood canal behind her trailer
ducks, egrets, and a single heron live along
the reedy banks; turtles, sometimes
an alligator, bass and the monster gar

swim the green dark water. The sky
is gray and full of gulls.
My mother is dying, morphine
in her veins, breathing ragged,

as if she's forgotten how, then remembers
with gasps and sputters.
My mother is dying. 3:34 a.m.
I hold her hand and fall

asleep. 4 a.m. My mother's dead.
Palm fronds rattle in the wind.
I walk the canal bank as the undertakers
drive her away. Later

I will remember this rain stinging,
the heron awkward as it lifts, falls, flies away.

Selling My Dead Brother

for Mick

I said yes to the phone solicitation
without much thought—he'd only
been dead a couple days. Why not use
his few good body parts

in some spooky transplant?
Most of his body had failed him:
eyes, crossed all his life, worsened
when diabetes set in. In his last years

he watched TV through binoculars.
His tongue too deceived him
into eating junk food washed down
by soda or sweet tea. His ankles

could not support his great weight.
His kidneys failed. The gout ate him alive.
It sounded noble, a gesture
I thought he might make, donate whatever

the compassionate phone solicitor
asked for. He fell for ideas like that.
When the thank you letter came
I saw my brother's body was an investment,

that I'd sold him to capitalist cartels at a price
he could never afford. Fault and blame?
He killed himself with too many plates
of pasta loaded with butter and Velveeta's

fake cheese. He washed everything down
with good ole Mountain Dew. The letter's
lost. I scattered his ashes at Clemente's
statue, Steelers field, the three rivers.

That was our life together. What more
could I have done before I signed him away?

An Abundance of Caution

For B & I

Because he knew what might save a life,
because the shiny hospital was just down the flat
wide street, because there were no IEDs,

because no one at the hospital
had a bomb strapped under her scrubs,
because no one hated him

and wanted him out of their country,
because all of this was so, he said
we're going to the emergency room.

His new wife said *it's just a little stomach
flu,* but she went anyway because
he'd bagged body parts and seen children

wasting on war torn streets. It
was her flu, but it was his story.
Because hospital staff didn't know

the story, they moved slowly,
muttered *there are people in here
who are really sick.* They sat

in uncomfortable chairs, and she felt worse
than at home. He was quiet as he tracked
everyone's movement—who looked innocent,

29

who could be dangerous. He watched
orderlies and nurses pass them by.
He knew how to be quiet, patient,

and he knew when to move. When he yelled
Medic. Someone, now, get over here.
Something in his voice, maybe

a desperate not here, not now, not again,
warned them and they came.

James Dickey Said

You have the hands of a piano player
and I said, yes, I play harmonica. He
laughed, said of course, and moved
on through the reception.

In a Laramie bar
by the railroad tracks
our band played nights
under a sky wide and high,
stars shining like a score

on the black sheets of heaven.
My hands fluttered. measured
the air it takes to bend a note
into the blue night stars.

There was no piano player
but when a freight rumbled through
the band left me to play wheels
on the tracks and a whistle
lost in the mountains west.

The Power of the Visible **Bought in a Used Book Store**

for Robert Dana

You wrote *to a book addict.*
I bought the book a few years later

The inscription—your bold scrawl,
flowing across the page like dinners

and drinks we'd have later in hotel bars.
That autograph said poetry could save us,

beauty might be enough to live on,
but if not we still had to try.

Not that you thought life
was easy. Some start off

in a difficult world and work,
love, or luck lead us to something

better. You had no reason to guess
he would fall so short. Let's say

he sold those promising textbooks
and then one day walked downtown

and looked in the bookstore window.
What did he see? A young woman home?

A hungry kid? Who is he now?
The old man at the laundromat

who said he didn't read poetry anymore,
and I didn't ask when he had.

Prose Poems

Forgetting the Nicene Creed

Father Mike was ecstatic. He'd looked at a convenience store
clerk and saw the Risen Lord and now he forgot to say the
Creed. Half the congregation knelt, half stood; I reverted to
catholic legalisms and wondered if this Mass—highest of all,
ritual of resurrection, cornerstone of faith, would count. What
if this topples the tower and this little church and its hundred
souls invalidate Easter. Jesus not risen? Stone not rolled away?
Mary M still weeping about a stolen body? There's a reason
for liturgy, I wanted to cry. You believe in one God. What now
about all things visible & invisible & Jesus—begotten not
made, of one substance w/the father? What of that? How after
you forget do you go back? It's not fair that I, who do not
believe in any of this anymore, should record thy fault. I used
to make up sins to confess when I'd yet to learn real ones, and
now I'm trapped with you, real sin on my soul and you forget
your Creed. He shall come back to judge the quick & the dead.
I may be among the quick *saying not me. I knew he should
have said it.*

Maybe this isn't sin, just Grievous Technical Fault, like when I
wore the orange stars and moon shirt to my Grandmother's
funeral. That wasn't held against her, I don't think, not me
either. Though who's to say what I would have become if
blessed. Rich? Famous? Handsome? A drummer in a rock and
roll band? I believed once in a holy, catholic & apostolic
church, though then I didn't know what apostolic meant. I
never looked for the resurrection of the dead. Maybe because
our priest was never excited, never so swept by passion that he
threw his arms open over all of us and cried *the Lord is Risen,
and we are all the Risen Lord*. I think this too was once a sin,

the Gospel of Thomas maybe. Too much *Kingdom of God is inside of you.* Too close to the pagan, made more for peace and love, not colonialism and manifest destiny.

What if Jesus is and is pissed? What if we blew it? This day's always been suspect in my book. Easter, the day you say He rose from the dead, rides our calendar like a rubber duck bobbing on carnival water. Moveable feast, we call it, to hide our confusion. If the Resurrection was going to be this fucking important, some scribe or apostle should have checked his day planner and jotted a note: *Jesus rose today*, not just some day after the spring equinox. Be more specific, for god's sake. That too, was not my doing. So should suddenly You become a wrathful god rather than a tad merciful, in case there's merit and consequence in all of this, the rite of the Eucharist, body & blood & magic, in case we are to follow ALL the rules, this one especially that they are toying with so cavalierly, in case you were thinking of smiting & smoting this little church to ash, please spare me and my family. We looked at each other, not as risen lords, but because we caught the error.

We were willing to say that You were incarnate by the Holy Spirit of the Virgin Mary, made man and crucified (for us), that you were buried & rose & ascended. I've been reading the Book of Common Prayer now for an hour. In case You were *thinking of feeding us the bread of tears, giving our crops to caterpillars, wiping us out of the book of the living, letting our enemies' dogs lick our blood,* remember (can you even forget?) it wasn't our doing. Ok, I don't Believe but I do believe that liturgy is liturgy. Yes, I've sung with too much glee Patti Smith's *Jesus died for somebody's sins but not mine.* Still, if Father Mike had said it, I would have remembered years of saying it and some of them in earnest. I still cringe a little when these Episcopalians add the extra words to your prayer our Father. No, I don't dwell in the shelter of the most high, but I have learned to number my days. I believe we might, at any time, be *swept away like a dream, fade suddenly like the grass. We are but flesh, a breath that goes forth and does not return.*

Wasn't This a Mighty Storm?

Rain it was a-falling/Thunder began to roll
Lightning flashed like hellfire/The wind began to blow

I'm standing on the 2nd story porch, wide enough for shelter
from the rain, wind blowing hard down the front of the house
and dark, dense, clouds massed just above the trees I'm calling
"tea olives" because it sounds so regional and plausible, and
feels a lot like Flannery O'Connor might live here too, though
I'm only a visiting writer (but she would be too and we would
be in residency together, and in this new fantasy would I be
more famous but less talented, or less famous and less
talented?) She would know that the trees high enough to be
bashed back and forth by the wind are not tea olives and would
no doubt point out, in a way that says remember, Mr.
Campbell, that despite your pretensions to knowing something
of the South, you are a Pittsburgh Yankee, and I would have to
admit that the trees in the wind are maybe beech, hickory,
white ash, live oak or some of the other many oaks that look
like the other Southern oaks. But the massed clouds do look
like clouds that spawn funnels, funnels that descend like
tongues of God (he has many, some small and pink like a
terrier's, some long and sticky like a frog's and the tornado
tongue that whirls faster and ever faster, sucking up all before
it and then battering it back to earth, smiting it, we might say
in a Biblical moment, that would lay low this little town that
does not have much left to lay low anyway, but lay it low still
like God's other wild wind tongues ripped through Tuscaloosa,
sundry parts of Alabama, Missouri, Georgia and God knows
where else this summer. My daughter watches tornado chasing
shows and she knows the numbers to measure destruction,

40

my chances of getting out of this Writer's Residency alive. My daughter would know better than I if a funnel is going to descend, and even if she wasn't sure she would surely say *Dad, get off the porch. Get in the house.* There's a basement here. She's longs for a basement to hide from tornados. She knows we are supposed to get in the bathtub, but we don't have bathtubs, and our bathrooms are on outer walls, so she's figured the closet would be the best place for us to crouch and pull pillows over our heads after we have gathered up all the dogs. Today, though she might know that this is just a storm and not a tornado, she might not be able to resist finally having a chance to huddle in a basement. Tornado or not I decide to put all the porch furniture on the lee side of the house, out of the wind (though I suspect if a tornado came this would prove silly) and then I come back to stand in stinging rain to watch the clouds race above those trees. Thunder finally triggers my fear of lightning and drives me inside. Flannery must have gone in long ago. Inside, I hear my residency host, who I imagined must be frightened by branches whipping the windows and the wind's low moan, playing the piano. I regret now my utter disregard of classical music because I'd like to say playing something Baroque, some Debussy, some romantic Schubert piece. I know enough not to say Wagner and I know we are not waltzing. I stand at the top of the stairs and the storm is louder than the music. I wonder if she plays like others pray—that the storm will spare her (us?), pass us over, leave the roof of this hundred year house intact; if she plays so her music will soothe the beast that this wind has become, has been since there was first wind and houses to ravage, beasts to fall upon us. I listen and think of the Titanic, of those British prisoners whistling the *Bridge on the River Kwai*, of someone fiddling while something burns, how these last long days I

41

have seemed transfixed before my own beast coming so steadily to find me. But I stay upstairs, walk into my room and turn on the computer to track the storm on Doppler radar. I zoom in and in and in again. This crossroads, this house between Royston and Hartwell, no zoom power can pinpoint us, is somewhere below the red furies that radar says are right upon us and I, given my time outside, must agree. Here I am now, obscured in the radar, in and of, here and there, part and parcel, flesh and pixel, man and computer, lost and found, hopeless and in despair. The red swirl moves away to the east, and outside the storm subsides too. This congruity satisfies, at least for now. No kicking the table to refute anything or anybody thusly. We seem safe unless there's a rogue gust trailing the storm, some ragged blackguard out to despoil and pillage our sodden villages. There might be a madman unhinged by the wind, bent on murdering the first people he comes across; our proximity to the railroad tracks could make us those people, but there's little to be done about that. I worry instead about the red fury heading toward the lake and hope the fishermen out there had enough sense to heed a siren somewhere sounding *seek shelter, turn your small boats toward home.*

Dates: A Meditation, 2015

To date: the infinitive form of the verb *date, dated, dating, had dated.*

First dates can go wrong for many reasons. Showing up
in your VW Microbus, knocking on her door
barefoot, shirtless, salt-bleached hair spilling
across your eyes and down your back as her mother
sizes you up: the potential dangers, the myriad things to worry
about if her daughter really gets in your bus, but she lets her date
you anyway and then worries more when she sees you crawl
under the bus with a screwdriver and jump the solenoid. A few
weeks later when you and her daughter get busted for possession
her worries are fully grounded; dating's done.

Dates: died, August 16th—Idi Amin, Shamu, Elvis, Bela Lugosi,
Babe Ruth, Margaret Mitchell, Robert Johnson, Andrew Marvell,
                    Kitty from Gunsmoke.
Born: Charles Bukowski, Frank Gifford, Lawrence of Arabia,
                    Fess Parker, Madonna, Ted Hughes.

Dates, from the Greek *daktulos* for "finger," fruit of a palm
native to Northern and Western Asia, provide sustenance.
Dates on Florida palms, however, can't be eaten. A trick
of the fruit God, who is beyond all dates in an eternity
of pears, figs, pomegranates and the deceitful apple
that begins the history of man, a date so important to Christian
theology that it has no date. Paradise is lost but Adam lives
begetting and begotting sons and daughters to birth the future sons
of Adam's sons who beget sons and daughters, killers, thieves,

the daughters of Lot and the men of Sodom who wanted to know angels carnally.

Genesis claims the Flood began on the 17th day of the 2nd month in Noah's 600th year when "the fountains of the great deep were broken up and the windows of heaven were opened." It rained, as most know, 40 days and 40 nights, then 150 days later the flood waters begin to recede. By October 1st on our calendar, Noah could see the mountains of Ararat and on January 1st the waters were dry and the Earth was reborn, but Noah was cautious and did not venture forth to celebrate. He stayed on the Ark, despite his pet dove bringing a fresh olive leaf, until on February 27th God couldn't take it anymore and told Noah, his family and the lucky animals, clean and unclean, to leave the Ark, be fruitful and multiply.

Adam's claymation begins what we could call history;
then like a middle school math story problem you add
the number of years Adam and sons live before begetting
more sons: 130 years, Adam begets Seth. 105 years later Seth
begets Enoch, so on and so on. Without showing all of the work,
my cell phone calculator says 1656 years pass between Adam
and the Flood and about 712 years between Abraham and Jesus.
This means Elvis left the building 4345 years after Adam's
fashioning.

Date, the point of time at which an event takes place,
from the medieval Latin *data*, feminine past participle of *dare*
meaning "to give." As in the Lord giveth and the Lord taketh away,
as in God says to Abraham kill me a son and Abraham says where
you want this killin' done? Out on Highway 61. April
Fools' Day, 2014, Blue Cypress Lake after midnight,
an owl in a Norfolk pine considers attacking my little dog and me
as we pee on the shell road in the light of a near full moon.
This day's record: no fish caught. Lost a favorite popping cork rig
in cypress roots. Saw two osprey, three hawks, and a blue heron.
Heard a gator bellow in the marsh and a limpkin cry.

In Pittsburgh, on October 13, 1960, at 3:35 on the scoreboard clock
Mazeroski hit a walk off homerun over Yogi Berra and the Forbes Field
wall to win the World Series. One day someone asked Yogi
"what time is it?" and he says, you mean now?

Parable of the Forest Pygmy

There's a story about a forest pygmy who's taken (not by force, but maybe tricked, not fully informed consent) out of the jungle canopy on to the savannah and he freezes, panics like a stoned hippie before a leering cop, then falls to the ground and covers his head. The space, the vastness of everything, the horizon stretching to the other end of the earth is too much for him. He's a level-headed, respected, experienced, worldly pygmy—a man among men in his own world and that's his problem. His known world, his points of reference, definition, boundary are gone and suddenly he's outside, exposed to who the hell knows what. There's only a finite number of things that can kill a pygmy in the jungle though it may seem ever so large when the killer comes: panthers, lions, snakes, even those ants that swarm down the trees and descend upon the more careless pygmies or more likely the foolish and uninformed European who got tired, or drugged on some exotic jungle berry juice. Even though a pygmy can't always see what's coming, at least he knows it's nearby. There's a learned level of alertness that will usually protect him and if the panther gets him anyway or he's trampled by the occasional but not totally random stampeding things that look like pigs, and maybe they are (a pygmy would know)— well, he tried. He can take small comfort knowing he was killed by a known danger, the same collection of dangers that killed many generations of his ancestors. As they say, in some more deterministic cultures, it was his time to go and the panther's time to eat. *But not this pygmy*. He's on the savannah, the plain, the plateau; he doesn't even have a name for it, even though it apparently has dozens of names. He can't even say what it looks like—flat, open, empty, sparse, desolate, bright, burnt sienna. He can't say gazelle, wildebeest, jackal, rhino, Jeep, Land

46

Rover. He probably has a word for dangerous, for fear, but it's too small for this. He probably even has a phrase for *oh shit what's that?* This pygmy just curls up in a ball, a fetal position; his anthropologist "friend" might, if he isn't a totally cruel jerk, gather the pygmy into his arms and say in a rough, but close enough for anthropology translation: "it's ok Frankie; it's just the savannah" (which as we know means nothing to poor Frankie) and lead him gently back to the cover of the panther and python filled forest. A grad student will be taking notes of course, or a film crew getting every touching and strange moment, but at least our pygmy will go home not too worse for wear, except for the lifetime of nightmares he will have where something silent and large comes out of the sky that never ends in a world where there's no place to hide and it's always too bright and burning and it snatches him up and he's gone, maybe forever, maybe just a night and then again the next night and the next.

47

English House Sparrows in the Consol Energy Center

Without question the most deplorable event in the history of American ornithology was the introduction of the English Sparrow.

-W.L. Dawson, *The Birds of Ohio*, 1903

They snuck in when the arena opened; loading dock doors beckoned the Sparrow, maybe a pair now and then, not some mad rush of starlings swooping along the river, so many that they look like the tattered flag of a country that's forsworn color. The House Sparrow—Old World import, the first Brooklyn birds captured, purchased, transported in cages—we ignored till they overran natives, ravaged crops, windowsills, and eventually, hockey arenas.

Our guide, Anthony, has become a sparrow expert of sorts; though not his primary mission, he's been charged to rid the arena of its unwanted guests, over two hundred now he guesses. He's learned much in his quest: the house sparrow's feeding habits, breeding habits, life span—but all of this comes to naught when he tries to kill them. What he learns is what's been learned. The House Sparrow adapts, takes what it needs from what we leave behind: popcorn, peanuts, chips, beer pooled in the hollows of the arena floors. Poor Anthony has been tasked with eliminating the *feathered rat*—had he read him no doubt he'd agree with Dodson:

The English Sparrow must go. The bird has wrought
a great deal of evil to our country chiefly. We
imported the English Sparrow— that was not
Nature's fault. We should rectify our error, drive out
the English Sparrow.

Anthony's considered many means of driving out the wily
birds that fly so blithely through the Consol sky. He's got a list
of failures. Antifreeze dough balls: the birds were too cunning
and popcorn too plenty. Cats—a cat's too smart to chase birds
high into girders, and if the odd dumb cats did, who would get
them down? The falconer decided one falcon couldn't kill
enough sparrows to scare the survivors away. Falcons hone
one target to scare the rest into fleeing or submitting. Falcons
are assassins, not mass murderers.

The English Sparrow's lifespan—Anthony doesn't like to call
them House Sparrows; he likes thinking of them as invading
from England like the Beatles—is twelve months in the wild,
twenty-four in captivity, but a hockey arena is the best of both
worlds. Sparrows are free to fly, feed, breed, live in a
temperate environment; no predators, except Anthony, and he
admits he's not been very predatory to date.

I offer this advice: *Anthony, this is going be harder than you think.* As one not bent on killing wrote, "house sparrows can live for several years if their needs are met." Some say they can live for two, four, maybe thirteen years. Do the math Anthony. Read and weep: "a few House Sparrows can multiply into thousands in a few years because they regularly raise three and sometimes as many as five broods per year, each brood averaging five or six birds." You might reduce their food supply by meticulously cleaning after every event, but your staff thinks it's doing that now; are you going to dun their wages for popcorn left in the aisles? Will they have to race sparrows to see who gets the peanuts first? You can't poison the popcorn; there's problems of liability and lawsuits if people start dying faster than sparrows.

You could blast disco at night with strobe lights, like PSY OPS went after Noriega, but who knows what freaks out a sparrow? Say no to flying trapeze performers catching birds with dip nets. Inefficient, and high liability if they insist on doing it without nets. Maybe you could drive them out if all 800 TV monitors show *Real Housewives of New Jersey* marathons, but sparrows might cultivate a certain weirdness and enjoy, especially, shows about stupid humans. Anthony, just count your blessings: I give you this Jubilate:

For sparrows are not pigeons,
For sparrows do not steal shiny baubles,
For sparrows bear no omens of death,
For sparrows do not eat dead flesh,
For sparrows are not loud as peacocks,
For sparrows do not excrete guano,
For *Sparrow is* not the nickname of a rival team,
For all of this, Anthony, you might rejoice.

If you stack all three of Albert Puhols' homeruns up
they would be higher than the tallest building in the
world.

I had a dream last night that I was trying to crash in a house
that I thought no one lived in. Maybe the owner lived
somewhere else most of the time like a middle-income
snowbird. A plain house, flat, sort of a modular design like
shipping containers stuck together without a thought of beauty.
It was on the flood control canal close to my mother's trailer
park. I wanted to crash there and leave no trace of my
marginally criminal existence. All I had with me fit in one bag;
one change of clothes, one bowl, one spoon, my pen knife.
Then the elderly Black woman who lived there came home. I
tried to hide behind the door as she came in but there wasn't
room. She was sad to have me arrested. I was one of her
children. My colleagues came to get me; they were driving my
little brother's gold Lemans convertible. They gave me lots of
time to gather my one bag of stuff and then we drove through
scenes of my life that never happened—occasions where I had
been kind strangers. There was an older man standing in front
of row of storage sheds who said I gave him something that
saved his life, and he asked if I remembered what it was.
Another man said this was where I changed the tire on a little
kid's bicycle. He opened his shed and showed me stacks of
army footlockers, each one filled with gold coins. When I
asked why, he just turned and moved on like the ghost of folly
past. Then I was telling the police that I was conducting a
sociology experiment, that I was here on a break from college,
that my mother lived right across the canal and I could have
gone home anytime. But she was already dead. One cop
seemed sympathetic, but he had to book me. Hardly anyone

really thought I should be arrested. I asked the jailer to tell the other prisoners that I was a professor and would help them write appeals and letters home. As I was about to be raped anyway, almost everyone agreed that was a shame too, sort of, but lives are what they are and choices have consequences. Everything that happens, they said, is what we have coming. I wanted to dispute their fatalism but thinking in large abstractions had become frightening and maybe I did have this coming. Suddenly I could see the pain entering my ass and I knew it would not kill me. Nothing would kill me. I wanted to apologize for my silly social experiment, but I woke and found myself living in the tallest building in the world that Albert Puhols had built last night. It was, as the commentator said, three towering homeruns high, a few feet taller than the Babe Ruth and Reggie Jackson Towers. Investors ran out of money. The skeleton was done but the interior never finished. Though I had lost my bowl at the old woman's house, I knew I could live here, use construction scraps to fashion shelter, make bowls from cans, a table from a bucket and a piece of plywood. I still had my knife. I'd be alone in the tallest building in the world. Albert's aloof, focused only on the next game. He won't care and he was not going to live here anyway. My friend, Good Danny, a Cardinal fan, might envy the iconic nature of my new fate: my life a mission, tribute, sacrifice to, or from, the gods of October. It wouldn't really matter because it was all an accident and true sacrifice must be intentional, thought out and played by the rules. All of this— Albert's indifference, Babe and Reggie's feats just waiting to be eclipsed, if only by a stupid statistic of how far in space three homeruns traveled, the present an estimate, the past a memory poorly measured, this too is how life works. Some guy on the radio makes an insignificant revelation, some other

53

guy outside a Catholic Church invents the Protestant religion, and we just keep going, trying again and again to live in houses we don't own. One bowl. One spoon. The human condition. This tower will do. No one here but me, no one likely to come up because the elevator's just a dark cold shaft that moans all night and descends into a hole in the earth below Texas. The world under Albert's home runs is unmapped, but it's not hard to imagine it as indifferent as the one we think of as home

Submission Guidelines

Do not submit poems that imitate
                       Allen Ginsberg.
Do not list demons. Control line length.
Commit no obscure Talmudic verses.
Do not chant; engage only in subtle repetition.
No gratuitous cursing. If you must say *fuck*
be hammering a nail, not writing a poem.
No insane asylums, no American Buddhism,
no unnecessarily long poems. The following words,
though not profane, should be avoided: *hysterical,*
naked, Mohammedan, Moloch, sutra, sunflower.
Pay no homage in supermarkets.
Play no small stringed instrument
                       or things with bells.

Searching for the God Particle

I suppose we would think there's only one,
a mono-God, one particle over all, everlasting,
though lost for eons, some incredible length

of God time, particle time, creation time,
but not eternity, because that's out of time.
This god particle, if found, might provide light

and warmth, or another weapon capable
of ending time as we know it and sending us
into the dark where even a God can't save us.

Imagine, till then, the God particle swinging
on strings through space like Tarzan on his vines,
and we too traversing this quantum universe with some,

but not Tarzanic, dexterity, haunted
by spooky actions at a distance, disappointed
by truths, fleeting; promises that expand

and collapse into new worlds of doubt.
Gods—Mighty and Merciful, Infinite,
Eternal, One and Many.

Waiting for Everyman

God him come and gone
and no man tricked
the one-eyed brute. Then

that guy, big man, washed
up on the beach. Folk
called him Esteban. Mayan,
maybe Guatemalan woman

today stood at the post office
window and pulled wrinkled
dollars from a baggie, bought

a money order. One story.
Where is it going? I stare
at the map, imagining

or remembering someplace
different. Dental hygienist
told me I had a sympathetic

tongue and cheek, tried
to protect me from cold
water's pain. I think yes

my tongue's known sympathy
and desire, my tongue's
danced in Rio and sleeps

too far from home. I am
waiting. No one knows
this but you.

What I Might Want Today

> "I suppose I would like more beauty"
> Kristen B, (of a poetry manuscript)

Yes, that and more freedom, love, wisdom,
generosity. More fish when I fish. More
runs for the Pirates, less for the other team,

More luck for my friends. More discipline
for me. Perhaps, in its way, more beauty
would accomplish all of this. Beauty,

as in elegance, grace—*there's a hole*
in daddy's arm where all the money goes/
Jesus Christ died for nothing I suppose.

All of this being, as they say, in the eye
of the beholder. If I lived dedicated
to the pursuit of beauty what old roads would I walk,

how parallel the roads to truth? Could I get
there from here, in this little poem? Yes,
because nothing is given?

Armadillo Crossing

Few care about them. Ok,
yes, the love of my friend's life
used to call him *my armadillo,*
but we figured that was more
metaphor than fact; though now
that she's gone he sometimes hides
in his shell. He's not armored
but tender if you find him out
in the world. Nature's beyond
our ken. No matter how carefully
we search it for meaning or hope.
The black bear took out the front end
of a Subaru when it crossed the road.
Armadillos and gators, though
the latter rarely cross the road,
do so without warning signs.
Slow children get our caution. Fast
children seem to take care of themselves
but often crash when they're grown.

The Bridge

A man looks down at the water, wonders how hard
it is. All the years of wading, walking the beach,
water soft, yielding, he's measuring wind,
strong from the northwest; he wonders how much
a falling object—a person—would drift
at this height given the wind's speed.

The man knows more about choices than he does
drift and water currents that drag a body toward the sea
some few miles away. He's not going to jump,
though it looks like he might. He's been here an hour.
He could have walked a green path in a meadow, stood
on a bluff watching prairie grass wave, listened
to a stream riffle white rocks and have thought, essentially,
the same thoughts. Not of falling, not the hard
pull of gravity, not the knots the wind blows,
but longer thoughts—where it begins,
where it ends. Not here.

Smack in the Middle of Nowhere

I was about to say that you have to wonder
where the middle of nowhere is, but of course
you don't. You might wonder about recovering
or dying from cancer or the brakes
on your car. Young mothers dying in the hospital. You
might wonder if your lover still loves you. Might wonder
if Trump or some other idiot will fuck up the world
beyond repair. You might wonder if its already
beyond repair.
                   But say you do wonder
about the middle of nowhere, not so much
where it is, but can nowhere have a middle?
Or maybe more cosmological, is there a nowhere?
Is it some deep space void thing beyond our
instruments' ken? If it's there do you know it
when you feel it—despair, loss, ennui? A place
worse than being No Man for real, not just
the product of O's wit, cunning, and guile.
I hope it's not some silly Zen thing like the sound
of one hand clapping, but maybe the Beatles
version—a Nowhere full of Nowhere Men. I'm supposing,
against logic, that it exists because I'm trying to find it,
sticking pins on a wall map. Idaho. Alabama. D.C.

Angels

Even an angel hits a stone wall
when the labors of angels

are no match for the grinding down
of lives in the human every day. Maybe

God tasked the angels to serve and protect us,
maybe Lucifer rebelled and caused a shit storm

to fall on us. Maybe there's no Lucifer
maybe there's no god, and the shit

is our own. A man locks three women
in his house, rapes them for years; a driver

tosses his dog into the highway
because another driver cuts him off.

White men in Texas pull a black man
behind their pickup truck and he dies

almost skinned. Cheney says water boarding
isn't torture. What angel could bear such things,

the worst that's happened, the worst that will?
An angel from Montgomery already sagging

under the burden of slavery, Jim Crow,
lynching, bombed churches? An angel

from Palestine? The angel of the Ovens?
The angel of tsunami? Ruwanda? Shiloh?

Nagasaki? Dresden? Wounded Knee?
We can't count on angels anymore.

The Mayor Says I Want That Sonnet by Tuesday

And so I labored. First just to conjure
something auspicious to give the octave
its proper potential. Lurking, hovering all
the time, the spectre of patterned rhyme.
He did not specify Italian or English.
Spenser's pretty much forgotten here.
Choosing between the two daunted my first slow steps.
I mumbled to my cats I'll get this done. Monday
then Tuesday gone, I worked in metric step,
let it bend my theme as it does. Dawn came.
The noises on the street, the village waking
to another day of toil cried you're running
out of time. So easy, I cursed, to offer
the obvious every time. End stops,

clichés stumbling over themselves like the peasants
that you are. Who was I talking to? No one's
ever there when the poet works. Oh, I wish
I had not agreed to this sinecure, that being
the village poet was not my trade. I could
have been somebody, a contender for a throne
who saved his words to advance selfish fortune
or woo women in taverns in other towns
with villanelles to soften their hearts. There was
one I desired, but I sold all for rent, meat and drink.
What did I know of this lonely office? We want
what we want and *want* is all we come to know.
This poem's due before the mayor's office closes;
his door says 5 pm, but everyone know he knocks

65

off early. I'll just give him the best I have. The idiot
wouldn't know a good poem if it bit him on the ass.
Mixed metaphors, slinking dactyls, fudged meter, just
work for hire. I'll get my money. He'll never fire
the only man dumb enough to take this job. Others
chop wood, dig their ditches, horde weeks for vacation,
count years till they retire. By three o'clock
I'll turn this crap in. Time to spare. Let the bastard
have his day. I'll twist him round once, twice;
may this malingering verse turn his soul to ice.
On the way back to my shack the road forks;
I'll take the one less traveled and pretend
it leads to love, then stop at the bar with the good porter.
Three porters, brave beer promises of revenge.

Fortified, I'll make more verses as I drink
and store them like nuts against my ruin.
When I can't live this unrequited life any longer
I'll hand the man a page: "verse libre," I'll say.
When he screams "this isn't a fucking poem"
I'll walk away for good and turn my hand
to prose. Flash fiction, for a start, short and sweet.
No rhyme, no meter, hell hardly even a plot.
Over before it begins. What could mean less?
Sure, there's worse a poet could do for money,
sell his words for ads, write political speeches.
I'll drift from town to town, barter my work
on cheap broadsides for meat, crackers and cheese.

Maybe read at a school here and there; winning
a little contest could sustain me as I roam.
A hundred bucks, a box of oranges, little rags
of flashy prose I'll give away for a song. Who
cares, now that the world's gone hollow and nothing
is as it seems? How many more stupid days before
I walk away, no verse I'm made to sing?
There are some who say I'll never leave, can't
hold my own in a world credentialed and defined.
I stare into my fire; deep in my cups I fear
they know me well. What measure can I summon
to sustain my longed for escape? My bravado
rings hollow when darkness thickens shadows here.
I consider all and turn my face from the mirror.

Red Nude Dreaming of Trout Fishing in Michigan

She's dreaming awake, on her knees,
elbows on a divan by the mahogany arm

of a red, hibiscus print couch. She looks
over her left shoulder at the painter and me.

Her ass, large, voluptuous, raises for a lover
to enter her like a stream pooling,

spilling over her black hair, her
red breasts, and the blue, blue divan.

Flying, Praying, Mourning

Of all the middle seats
on all the planes flying
today, this man, smelling
metallic and stale, sits next
to me. He moans, gargles,
mutters. He holds his head
in his hands. What afflicts him?
Can he pass it to me? Is he the foil
to my earlier lucky find—the largest
priest I've ever seen. 6-6, 260,
fair-haired, pink-skinned. Thirty years ago
a tackle at Notre Dame. But oh Mother
Mary, will he or you save me now?

Seashore

Some of us were caught sleeping, others
looking the wrong way. Ghost crabs belly up.
Hermit crabs hoarding water in whorled
shells. We should have paid more attention to the sea,
tide and time. We watched early morning walkers,
too sure of ourselves, our instincts, our
peculiar talents. The neap tide left us lost
and what we found was more desert than shore.
Maybe we were lulled by the everyday news of the sun
and wind, the moon's coming back again and again.
Did we attend irrelevancies, or is this the way things are?
Too late to debate determinism—the horseshoe's twenty feet
from the water's edge, periwinkles gasp below the sand.
Our stories end here: for crustaceans no resurrection,
rapture or repair. We left that to those who needed it,
and now we wonder at our lonely wisdom.
The gulls are winging in.

Reckoning

The morning moon, seven kinds of trees, one
white beech, nine shining branches spreading
like a candelabra. Hawk, rooster, crow,
a clutch of songbirds. Four squirrels, one traversing tree
tops, leaping from the frail end of one branch
to the frail beginning of another, back
and forth, back and forth, back and forth.

He's not a lightweight swinger of birches,
but a rasper of sweet gum and oak. I tell myself
the story of the last time I woke happy, distract
myself with listing what I did not do last night but meant to.
What kept me up till early morning
since I graded no papers and wrote no poems? The Tigers
lost, and with that my frail chance of going to the World Series.
Oregon in their ugly uniforms beat Arizona
in the middle of our Eastern night, but I did not care.
I mark the hawk again, its nest dark in morning shadows.
I measure the pain in my back against the weeds still
to pull on my hands and knees. I would be a pilgrim
and crawl through the medieval streets to you, but
this morning I am whirling, trifling, truant.

Another List of Things I Have Attended to Sloppily

The wheelbarrow's mismatched handles,
one sideways so that it's narrower
                              than its mate.

The garden gates, once my pride, now
slanted, ajar, hinges rusted and failing.

The rails of Della's tree house
that somehow escaped their nails.

The driveway, forever rutted,
waiting its promised gravel.

The Chinaberry trees, invaders
that grow like weeds.

The red heeler who so hates a bath.
The gutters—pine straw and dirt
                              turned to mulch.

The roof, compromised, its leaks.
The front doorknob rattling, loose,
                              that one day will

fail to let me in. The unspoken
that can never be repaired.

Fisherman at Boat Ramp

A man in green bibs
raises a working
wave, climbs into his skiff.
Mullet nets heaped
on the bow, he kicks
his motor over and diesels
off into the bay. I hear
him after he's gone

My weather app says
ten percent chance of rain
today. Seventy percent
at ten a.m. No time
like the present I turn
for home and walk as fog
turns to drizzle, contemplate
the uncertainty of math
and predictions.

The World Can Break Your Heart with its Forever

from Julia B. Levine

On & on it goes
when it stops
nobody knows.
I live alone, my dog
in his dog years
enters his 7th decade.
I am deep into my 6th. Outside
the back door the sun
rises over pines.
Behind them, unseen, the Gulf
of Mexico, stretches
into clouds.
I could be a bird today
a swift who flies
into the almost
forever, ten months on the wing.
That's romantic tripe.
I'm stuck here. Closest
I get to flying is speeding over the bay's
high arched bridge
looking down
at the braided river currents
as they break round
oyster bars.

When I cross the bay, I tell the person
who could be next to me
this is my place
where river, bay, and gulf
become one. It's a quiet
conversation, yes
but a comfort, the way,
the way all the known world
agrees with me.

The Dance

for Michelle Boisseau

She pulled me out into the middle
of the floor; the middle was always
hers. Half the people in the room
danced from memory no matter
what the song. I was among
that number. Mid floor was illuminated
by the awkwardness we make
when we think too many are watching us
be the fool too many are. Tonight
they were watching her as I flailed
and failed to follow her lead. What song,
I can't recall, but it was old. Halfway
through the second chorus I realized
that no gyration, no twirling arm she thrust
toward me or the disco ball
had anything to do with the beat.
I was drowning out there when a woman
I barely knew said *may I have him.*
Fast and firm, she took my arm
before my companion could say no
and pulled me out of the rip tide.
Then I caught a shore break; I spun
and spun again, shuffled like Travolta's
Michael discovering how wonderful it was
to dance like humans do.

For the Christmas Dead

Snoopy, Santa, the Snowman
sprawl on the ground, dusted
by last night's snow. Reindeer crumple
belly up, legs twisted.
One can imagine wolves close
to the door. Gray dawn backlights
the black elm; crows strafe
the porch, target the French doors
that I lay behind wrapped in blankets.
My lover declared we are safe in this house
and I wondered what she dreamed.
In Syria, Yemen, Paradise, the dead
are always dead; crows sing
O Come O Come Immanuel.
There's no sign that he will. I rest
my head on her sleeping shoulder.

Woke Up Holding the Moon in My Hands

The alligator calls the dog
The trash can calls the bear
The hawk calls the rabbit
The car calls the deer
Sorrow calls us home

Trailers call the hurricane
Lowlands call the flood
The shooter calls us to the mall

Prayers call God to save us
God calls from far away
Can't cross over, the water's
                  too high

**You're so vain you probably thought this poem
was about you.**

for Alice

I did. I thought this could be me.
I knew it was you too. Not you
& me, long friends, but never
tossed together by *Aphrodite's urge.*
Still, I was never out of it because it was about love
& loss & betrayal; repentance & our stubborn
will to accept what's been done as affirming the heart's
wild desire, even though that desire wrecked much
of what we held dear. We succumb to what
our heart and body crave. We live in the world
we've made, or remade, not without regret,
but our regret does not wall off the world we want.

We say we're sorry & we mean it.
We think our friends & even those we love
who we've hurt will forgive us because we love—them
& us & others & love itself.
We're delusional, yes.
We should have lived our lives with warning signs:
Detour Ahead. Bridge Ices before Road Surface.
Maybe no words, just swerving parallel lines
on a yellow field, that to others says *Caution,
Danger*, but we see a dance of long-stalked daisies
swaying in the wind. And there it is, our accident
coming toward us, unknowing, trusting, open.

About the Author

Rick Campbell is a poet and essayist living on Alligator Point, Florida. He's published six other poetry collections, as well as poems and essays in numerous journals including *The Georgia Review*, *Fourth River*, *Kestrel*, *Prairie Schooner*, and *New Madrid*. He's won a Pushcart Prize and a NEA Fellowship in Poetry. He teaches in the Sierra Nevada University MFA Program.